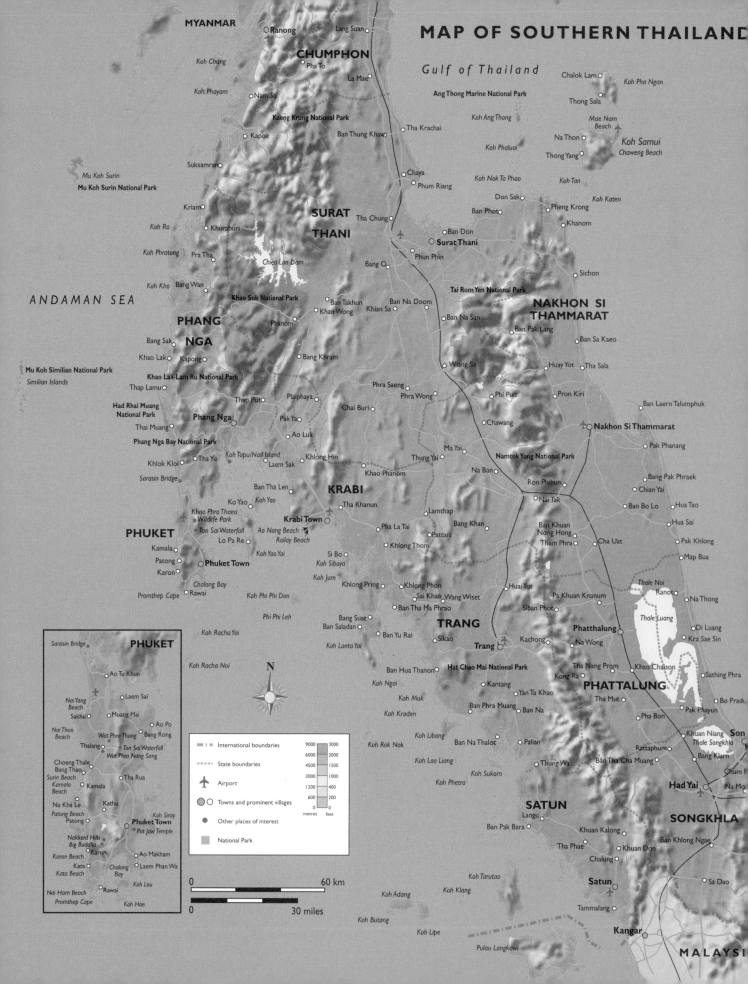

ENCHANTING
PHUKET
SAMUI & KRABI

MICK SHIPPEN

Contents

Above left: A 'katoey' or transvestite performing in a popular Phuket cabaret.

Above centre: Kata Beach, Phuket.

Above right: Wat Chalong, one of Phuket's most revered Buddhist temples.

Opposite: Koh Tapu or Nail Island, more commonly referred to as James Bond Island.

Title page: The huge standing Buddha image atop a hill in Had Yai Municipal Park.

Chapter 1: Thailand's Tropical Paradise

When the first backpackers washed up on the beaches of southern Thailand, they must have thought they had discovered true paradise. Little more than four decades ago, most of the coastline was dotted with traditional villages, the waters fished by sea gypsies and the islands deserted. But word soon spread and, awakening to the potential of its remarkable natural assets, Thailand opened her arms and warmly welcomed a burgeoning number of tourists. Within a remarkably short period, the region developed into one of the world's most popular holiday destinations. And so it remains.

Today, millions of tourists, both local and international, have discovered the astonishing natural beauty of Phuket, Koh Samui, Krabi and other highlights of southern Thailand, with many returning year after year lured by the azure waters, white sand beaches, friendly people, vibrant entertainment, delicious seafood and much more besides.

It is undeniable that Phuket and Koh Samui have both become victims of their own success. In many places they suffer the effects of uncontrolled development and mass tourism due to the government's reluctance to curb the growth of Thailand's cash-cow. But this is far from a case of 'Paradise Lost'. There is now, at long last, a growing awareness of the importance of a more sustainable approach to tourism, and while that may be too late for centres like Patong Beach on Phuket or Chaweng Beach on Koh Samui, many destinations are now attracting visitors who are not only interested in the beach life but are also coming for an enriching experience through nature, adventure and culture. And that's the real beauty of southern Thailand. It has something for everyone.

Each year, sailors drop anchor for a week to compete in the Phuket King's Cup Regatta, one of Thailand's biggest and most prestigious sporting events, and, just a few hours' boat journey from the island, top dive sites attract scuba divers from around the world. In Krabi, daring beginners and seasoned pros scale the sheer cliffs of Railay Beach and numerous other craggy limestone formations, while others discover unique wildlife habitats in the mangrove forests and mountains. Those seeking sanctuary find respite from the world by retreating to the seclusion of an exclusive resort or private villa or hire boats that whisk them to deserted beaches where they can feel like theirs is the first foot to leave its imprint in the soft white sand. Culture buffs can uncover a fascinating past in Phuket Town, while foodies can embark on a culinary journey that includes bustling markets bursting with intriguing ingredients and eat at street stalls and shophouse restaurants whose distinctive local cuisine also serves as a living link to the region's history and migration.

Tourism in the south continues to evolve, welcoming new visitors for new experiences. Beach bum, party animal, culture vulture or high flyer with a taste for the good life, Phuket, Koh Samui, Krabi and southern Thailand ensure a memorable stay in one of Asia's most beautiful regions.

Opposite: Built into the hillside overlooking the ocean, the Banyan Tree Samui is one of the island's most luxurious resorts. Guests enjoy pool villas and a secluded private beach.

Above: After years of neglect, many of the historic shophouses in Phuket Town are now being restored and finding a new lease of life as boutique guesthouses, coffee shops and art galleries.

Geography and Climate

B ounded by the Gulf of Thailand to the east and the Andaman Sea to the west, southern Thailand is an elongated peninsula with a rolling landscape and tropical rainforest. The region covers 70,000 km² (27,027 sq miles) divided into 14 provinces, the most southerly of which – Satun, Songkhla, Yala and Narathiwat – border Malaysia.

Phuket (pronounced *poo-ket* not *foo-ket* as many tourists mistakenly say) is Thailand's largest island with an area of 930 km² (360 sq miles), making it roughly the size of Singapore. Located in the Andaman Sea, 840 km (522 miles) from Bangkok, Phuket lies off the country's western coast. The island is approximately 50 km (31 miles) long and 15 km (9 miles) wide, and linked to the mainland in the north by Sarasin Bridge. To the north of the island are the renowned destinations of Khao Lak and Phang Nga, while Krabi lies to the east and Koh Phi Phi to the south-east. Koh Samui and Koh Pha Ngan lie off the country's east coast in the Gulf of Thailand.

The west coast of Phuket has the most beautiful beaches including Patong, Karon, Kata, Kamala and Surin, often separated from each other by rocky headlands. The attractiveness of the beaches and the quality of the sand have meant that most of the island's resorts and nightlife are to be found here. The eastern coast, on the other hand, is less physically appealing but has proved to be an excellent location for the island's marinas. Phuket International Airport is located in the north of the island.

Right: *Southern Thailand's beautiful coastline.*

Right: Much of southern Thailand is made up of a rugged landscape covered with lush rainforest.

Opposite: Loved by some, loathed by others, Phuket's Patong district has undergone fast and uncontrolled development.

Below: Traditional fishing boats moored in a sheltered bay in Krabi province.

In Phuket's interior the hilly landscape rises to 500 m (1,640 feet) and includes several protected and heavily forested areas. In the lowlands there are many rubber and coconut plantations, once providing an important occupation for islanders but now increasingly side-lined by tourism.

Situated to the south-east of the island, Phuket Town is the commercial centre and, despite the recent boom in modern development, it is still home to some splendid examples of Sino-Portuguese architecture. Although most visitors opt for resort and beachfront accommodation 16 km (10 miles) away, those with an interest in history and culture will find a couple of nights spent in Phuket Town to be extremely rewarding.

Climate

Southern Thailand has two major seasons: the rainy season with sporadic downpours starting in May and steadily building to a peak in September and October and the hot season from November through until April, which is also the peak tourist season, when the average temperature ranges between 22 and 34 degrees Celsius (72 and 93°F).

Although visitors should not be deterred by the rainy season (especially as there are many accommodation bargains to be had), it isn't the best time to come if you are interested in scuba diving as the waters can be choppy and less clear.

A Brief History of Phuket and Southern Thailand

Evidence of human habitation dating back to prehistoric times has been discovered in caves in southern Thailand. The most significant find was at Tam Lang Rongrien in Krabi province. Excavated in 1983 by the American archaeologist, Douglas Anderson, the cave yielded an exciting collection of primitive stone tools believed to date back 38,000 years.

It is known that Indian traders arrived in southern Thailand in 600 BC and introduced Hinduism to the region. Chinese merchants were also present in the area by 230 BC during which time Thailand was part of Funan, a kingdom that also encompassed parts of present-day Cambodia, Laos and Vietnam.

From the 7th to the 13th centuries the kingdom of Srivijaya ruled southern Thailand and Malaysia, with the upper states embracing Buddhism and the far south turning to Islam. By the turn of the 13th century, however, the influence of Islam had started to spread northwards to Pattani and Songkhla, and displaced Buddhism as the main religion.

The provinces of Songkhla, Pattani, Narathiwat, Yala and Satun were not part of Thailand until annexed by Rama V in 1902 in order to prevent losing parts of the south to the British, the colonial powers in Malaysia at the time. In 1909 an Anglo-Siamese Treaty was signed and the border with Malaysia was fixed. However, with their Islamic faith and Malay dialect, the people of these provinces always harboured a deep distrust of the Thai government and in 1957 a guerrilla army, led by the Pattani United Liberation Organisation or PULO, began fighting for a separate Muslim state. Following peace talks and the promise of limited autonomy for the south, the situation improved during the 1990s but flared up again in 2001 as a result of controversial policies carried out during the prime ministership of Thaksin Shinawatra. In provinces where up to four-fifths of the population are Muslim, the region's history sits uneasily with the present. Since 2004 regular shootings and bombings that target government institutions and Buddhists have claimed more than 5,000 lives. With a strong military presence and the constant threat of insurgent attacks, visitors to Thailand are advised to avoid the far south, especially the provinces of Pattani, Yala and Narathiwat.

On December 26, 2004, at the peak of Thailand's tourist season, Phuket and the western coast of Thailand felt the full and devastating force of a tsunami. The Thai government reported 4,812 confirmed deaths, 8,457 injuries and 4,499 missing. One of the worst-affected areas was Khao Lak, a long strip of beach lined with resorts and restaurants 80 km (50 miles) north of Phuket. Such was the destructive power of the wave that at the time it seemed it would take the country years to recover. However, less than a year later many resorts were back in business and welcoming tourists who were eager to show their support for the resilient Thai people. Today, the coastline has tsunami-detection buoys and alarm towers to ensure adequate warning can be given if earthquakes trigger a tsunami, and clearly signposted evacuation routes are in place.

History of Phuket

The earliest known reference to Phuket can be found in the writings of the Roman geographer, Ptolemy. In the 3rd century AD he mentioned an island called Jang Si Lang (later referred to by the corruption, Junk Ceylon). Prized for its abundance of tin and gems, the island became part of the kingdom of Siam in the 13th century. Three centuries later, the Dutch were lured by Phuket's valuable natural resources but they were not the only Europeans keen to exploit its wealth. In 1681, the French appointed a governor on the island and the British, who wanted to establish a base close to the Straits of Malacca, temporarily settled on Phuket before moving on to the more strategically important island of Penang off the coast of Malaysia.

In 1767 an invading Burmese army sacked the capital of Siam, Ayutthaya, before advancing southwards to Phuket. Warned of the impending attack by the British naval officer, Captain Francis Light, the Burmese army was repelled and Phuket remained under the control of Siam.

It was Dutch and Portuguese traders, and the Chinese settlers they brought with them, who exerted the greatest influence on Phuket. The island's naturally sheltered position in the Andaman Sea provided safe anchor for merchant ships sailing from India to China, while the tin mining boom of the 19th century attracted thousands of Chinese labourers to the island. This massive influx of immigrants shaped Phuket's cultural and architectural landscape. Old Phuket Town is still dominated by families of the original Chinese settlers, temples are scattered across the island and the annual festivals, including the huge vegetarian festival, reflect Chinese not Thai culture.

The growth of tourism

Today, Phuket is one of the most popular tourism destinations in Asia. It's almost hard to believe that it was only as recently as the early 1970s that the first simple beach bungalows opened on Patong, now a built-up area with a reputation as a no-holds-barred party town. Initially, the island's first visitors were adventurous backpackers who had heard tales of near-deserted beaches and a crystal-clear sea scattered with emerald islands. But when the airport opened in the mid-1970s, the numbers of European visitors increased year-on-year and Phuket began its rapid, often uncontrolled development as it transformed into Thailand's tourist hotspot. In 2019, Phuket Airport handled a record 11 million international passengers. The figures also show a drop in Europeans and strong growth from China and Russia, the result of the Tourism Authority of Thailand's efforts to attract new markets.

Opposite: A Chinese-style stone carving at Jui Tui temple. The influence of early Chinese settlers is evident across the island but strongest in Phuket Town.

Above: Thai Hua Museum on Krabi Road in Phuket Town, a former school and an impressive example of Sino-Portuguese architecture.

The People

The official resident population of Phuket is around 400,000 but, swollen by a huge influx of transient Thais and migratory Burmese workers who are drawn to the island to work in the tourist industry, the actual figure is thought to be closer to 1.2 million. There is also a significant number of expatriates from around the world who have made the island their home.

Culturally, the two ethnic groups that have had the greatest influence are the Chinese and the Thai Muslims. Unlike Bangkok's Chinese migrants who were mostly Teochew from the Guangdong region, Phuket's settlers were Hokkien from southern Fujian, as were those in neighbouring Malaysia and Singapore. Many of the early arrivals found work as labourers, worked in the rubber plantations and tin mines or sold noodles. As has been the case throughout much of Southeast Asia, however, they integrated into the local population by marrying Thais. The first generation born to Thai-Chinese families were called Hokkien Baba and successive generations have managed to preserve a strong cultural identity which is clearly visible today in Chinese religious practices, traditions and cuisine across the island but particularly in Phuket Town. As in Bangkok, the Thai-Chinese came to dominate Phuket's business sector with many early settlers becoming rich merchants who built grand mansion houses. Today, the Thai-Chinese population on the island is more than 40 per cent.

Around 35 per cent of Phuket's population is of Malay descent, and their Muslim culture and cuisine add another layer of interest and flavour to island life. Traditionally, the majority of the Thai-Muslim population on Phuket have worked as rubber and rice farmers, and as fishermen. In Thailand's southernmost provinces of Pattani, Narathiwat and Yala, the Muslim majority speak a Malay dialect.

Sea Gypsies

Thailand's Andaman coast is also home to an ethnic minority known in Thai as the *chao lay*, the sea gypsies. As the name suggests, these indigenous people once lived as nomadic fishermen. There are an estimated 12,000 sea gypsies in Thailand, comprising three different ethnic groups: the Urak Lawoi, Moken and Moklen. They are thought to have come from the Andaman and Nicobar Islands between Thailand and India. A dark-skinned people with curly black hair, they speak their own languages and have an animistic belief system.

Since Phuket's dramatic development as a top tourist destination, the sea gypsies have been increasingly marginalized and feel that their unique culture and way of life are at risk. Although they still make a meagre living as fishermen, many have settled in beachfront communities, one of which is at Rawai on the south-eastern tip of the island and at Koh Sirey, just east of Phuket Town. Although the government passed a resolution in 2010 that aims to protect their way of life, they claim it has made little difference to their plight and attempts to evict the landless people from their homes by developers are common.

A Haven for Retirees

Phuket's booming tourist industry and buoyant property market have brought the island huge prosperity. The island boasts one of the highest per capita incomes of any province in Thailand but it is also one of the most expensive places to live. Phuket is now known as a location for second homes for wealthy businessmen from Hong Kong and Singapore, and a haven for retirees keen to escape cold European winters.

In recent years, Phuket has also attracted large numbers of migrants from neighbouring Myanmar. Lured by a better income than in their home country, they have found employment on construction sites, in restaurants and bars, and as casual labour.

Opposite: The Malay influence can be seen in crafts, such as batik, which is used to decorate sarongs.

Above right: In Krabi Town a good way to explore the waterways, fishing villages and mangroves is to hire a local fisherman.

Right: A 'chao lay' or sea gypsy making a fishing basket. In Thailand's tourism hotspot, sea gypsies struggle to maintain their traditional way of life.

Religion

Opposite: Wat Chalong is considered Phuket's most important Buddhist temple and is also the island's most popular with both Thai and foreign visitors.

Below left: The marble-covered Big Buddha at the top of the Nakkerd Hills.

Although predominantly Buddhist, southern Thailand also has an evident Muslim influence which is particularly strong in rural areas and the provinces bordering Malaysia. In the main towns where Chinese families dominate the economy, Taoist shrines abound. It all makes for a colourful and fascinating cultural landscape for visitors.

Buddhism

Though Buddhism has the largest number of followers, at 73 per cent this is less than other parts of Thailand. As you would expect, many of the 38 temples on the island of Phuket, more than half of which are in and around Phuket Town, feature Chinese Buddhist imagery. There are also many small shrines tucked away down side streets to discover. Important Buddhist temples within Phuket town include Jui Tui. The revered Chinese temple has a central role during the island's Vegetarian Festival (see page 23).

Crowning a 400-m (1,312-ft) peak in the Nakkerd hills between Chalong and Kata, Big Buddha is Phuket's most well known and most visited landmark. The 45-m (148-ft) image, clad in white marble and seated upon a giant podium of lotus leaves, has been a work in progress for many years and is being financed entirely through donations. Visitors enjoy 360-degree views of the beaches below.

Second only to the Big Buddha in popularity is Wat Chalong. The temple has two floors and houses 36 Buddha images. It is also the location for a statue of Luang Pho Cham, who helped the people of Phuket suppress the Angyee, or Chinese Coolie Rebellion in 1876.

Wat Phra Thong in the Thalang district is one of the largest temples in Phuket. It is renowned for the Luang Poh Phra Thong, a golden Buddha image that looks like it is emerging from the earth. The oldest temple on Phuket is Wat Phra Nang Sang. Dating from 1785, its claim to fame is

Above left and right: Details of Wat Chalong.

Right: Many of the Taoist shrines have collection of beautiful images that are paraded around the town during the annual Vegetarian Festival.

Opposite top: Buddhist monks collecting alms in Had Yai.

Opposite below: Beautiful carvings inside the Shrine of the Serene Light in Phuket Town.

that it was once used as a fort to help protect the island against the Burmese invasion. The old chapel also houses three large Buddha images made of tin, each of which has a smaller Buddha in its stomach.

Thai Muslims

The majority of Phuket's large Muslim population are concentred in the Surin area where the original Malay migrants settled. Despite being a minority compared to the Thai Buddhists, mosques outnumber temples. There are 52 mosques including 31 in the Thalang district, 14 in Phuket Town and seven in Kathu district.

Chinese Taoists

Put Jaw Temple, the oldest Chinese Taoist temple on Phuket is located next to Jui Tui Temple. Built over 200 years ago, Put Jaw is dedicated to Guan Yin, the Goddess of Mercy, who is revered by Taoists as an immortal.

Food

ach region of Thailand has its own distinct culinary traditions and renowned dishes. Phuket and the south are no exception. The food, particularly in the far south, is strongly influenced by Muslim culture, while in Phuket Town and other main commercial centres, Thai-Chinese cuisine is more common. The region's bountiful and varied catch of seafood also plays a starring role in vibrant local markets and on the tables of many restaurants.

Fire and Spice

The Muslim-influenced southern Thai food carries much of the trademark pungency of Indian cuisine, and is heavily spiced making it much hotter than Thai food from other regions. One famous southern Thai dish is *massaman* curry. Deriving its name from a corruption of Muslim, this dish, more than any other, points to the strong influence of migrants. This delicious curry uses dried and roasted spices, such as cinnamon, cloves, cardamom and cumin, to create a rich, dark and fragrant curry of lamb, goat or chicken, which is traditionally served with *roti*, an oily, pan-fried bread that also originates in India. *Roti* is also eaten in the south in the form of *martabak*. The flatbread is stuffed with curried chicken, beef or fish, folded into a square and fried on a hotplate. *Roti* can also be eaten as a dessert when it is

Above: Southern Thailand's vibrant fresh markets offer a fabulous choice of exotic ingredients.

Above right: A small shop in Phuket Town making 'roti', a Thai Muslim bread often served with curry.

filled with a mixture of banana and egg, rolled up and drizzled with sweet condensed milk. Delicious but not for the calorie-conscious diner.

The most widely known southern meal is *khao mok gai*, steamed yellow biryani rice with chicken. Often served with fried shallots, a sweet sauce and a clear *tom yam* broth, the satisfying dish is a lunchtime favourite with many Thais.

Other popular southern dishes include *gaeng tai pla*, a tasty and often highly spiced dish made from the innards of fish. *Gaeng som*, a sour fish curry with a deep yellow colour from a mix of red chillies and turmeric, is another regional favourite. A bitter vegetable popular in the south is *sa-tor*, also known as 'stink bean' due to its pungent aroma. The large green seeds grow on trees in long wavy pods and are commonly fried with red curry paste and shrimps in a dish known as *pad ped sa-tor*.

Left: The distinctive southern, spicy Thai cuisine is a delight for adventurous eaters.

Above: For those who can't handle the heat, resorts offer more familiar fare.

Chinese Influence

Chinese dishes are very much part of the Thai food scene. In Phuket and elsewhere in southern Thailand, diners can enjoy old-style Hokkien noodles or *Hokkien mee*. Served as a noodle soup or dry with a soup on the side, this complex and flavourful dish of yellow egg noodles is dressed with a dozen ingredients including crabmeat, shrimp, fried shallots, peanuts, beansprouts, fresh chilli and white pepper.

Thai Seafood

High on the list of Thai culinary passions is seafood. The extensive coastline of the southern peninsula is scattered with tiny fishing villages and thousands of boats set out to sea at dusk, returning to shore at first light with their catch.

The majority of Thai restaurants will feature a substantial section devoted to seafood dishes, and there are also many restaurants that specialize in seafood. Classic dishes include

pla nueng manaow, steamed sea bass cooked in a spicy lime sauce, and *tom yam bpo taek*, literally 'broken fish trap soup', a sweet, sour and spicy soup that usually contains shrimp, fish, squid and clams. Deeply satisfying, this dish is comfort food at its best. Another favourite is *hoy lai pad nahm prik paow*, small clams flash-fried in a mild and flavoursome roasted chilli paste and a handful of Thai basil, the perfect accompaniment to a *tom yam*.

Left: Hokkien-style noodles, the complex and flavourful dish of yellow egg noodles dressed with a dozen ingredients.

Opposite top left: Kwiteow lod', Chinese-style stuffed noodles.

Opposite top right: Khao yam' is a delicious southern-style rice salad and a must-try dish. The rice is often coloured with butterfly pea flowers which gives it a delicate hint of blue.

Opposite below: Stir-fried clams with roasted chilli paste and Thai basil, one of a seemingly endless repertoire of seafood dishes available in the south.

Festivals and Events

Southern Thailand has a varied calendar of colourful festivals and events throughout the year. Many are actively promoted by the Tourism Authority of Thailand with the biggest and brashest taking place in Phuket.

Chinese New Year

Celebrations for Chinese New Year are extremely important for the Chinese community on Phuket and in large commercial centres such as Had Yai and Surat Thani. In common with many cultural festivals held throughout Thailand, the exact date varies from year to year and is determined by the lunar calendar. Festivities last for several days in late January or the first half of February during which time many Chinese businesses close so that people are free to clean their houses, feast with family and friends, and visit the temple.

Songkran New Year

Thai New Year, or Songkran, a national festival, is one of the most exuberant on the local calendar. The festivities, which involve religious rites and huge water fights from dawn until dusk, take place nationwide for several days with Songkran Day being celebrated on April 13. In Thai, Songkran means 'move' or 'change place', hence the festival marks the time when the sun changes its position in the zodiac. The associations with water are connected to the belief that people can wash away their bad luck of the past year.

Right: *Songkran or Thai New Year takes place in mid-April, the hottest time of year, when a heat-stressed population cools off during a three-day water fight.*

Opposite: *During the annual Vegetarian Festival, images from Taoist shrines are paraded through the town.*

Por Tor Hungry Ghost Festival

In September, the Chinese community celebrate the annual merit-making festival of Por Tor or Hungry Ghosts. (The act of giving earns 'merit', essential for spiritual growth.) According to believers, it is during this time that spirits return to roam the earth, so they are given offerings of food, including *ang ku*, red cakes in the shape of a turtle which are said to bring good luck, as well as paper money, candles and flowers. On Phuket, the largest celebration takes place at Por Tor Kong Shrine near Phuket Town and Seng Tek Bew Kuan Im Tai Seu Shrine in Bang Neaw district. Again, events are scheduled according to the Chinese lunar calendar so dates vary from year to year.

Vegetarian Festival

The annual Vegetarian Festival takes place all over Thailand in October but Phuket is renowned for holding the biggest event. Held over a ten day period, it is also one of Thailand's most gruesome and is not for the faint-hearted as it features stomach-churning, ritual face and body piercing with a bizarre variety of objects. The procession also includes images of Chinese gods that are carried through the streets while evil spirits are kept at bay by the startlingly loud bang of firecrackers.

The origins of the festival date back to 1825 and reflect the history of Phuket's large Chinese community. Legend has it that the festival, which is known as Jae Chai in

Hokkien dialect, began when a visiting Chinese opera troupe fell sick from fever. In order to honour two of the gods, Kiew Ong Tai Teh and Yok Ong Sone The, they decided to become vegetarian and as a result the troupe recovered. At the time Phuket was entirely covered with dense forest and fever was common, claiming the lives of many of the Chinese immigrants, most of whom worked in the tin mines. Hearing of the miraculous recovery, the people of Kathu district took to the vegetarian diet and the festival began.

Today, the festival attracts huge crowds and is a highlight of the Phuket calendar. Buddhists taking part have to adhere to ten strict rules which include abstaining from eating meat, from drinking alcohol and from having sex for the duration of the festival.

Jazz and Blues

Phuket Jazz and Blues Festival is an occasional event which brings together dozens of the best of Thailand's musicians and some international artists. The popular one-day festival is usually scheduled for December, when the weather is cooler. Jazz and blues fans can relax on the beach with great music and an array of tasty food and drinks. Throughout the rest of the year, Phuket has a lively music scene and there are many venues in the beach resorts, as well as in Phuket Town, hosting talented acts.

Loy Kratong

Renowned as one of Thailand's most beautiful festivals, Loy Kratong takes place in every town and village on the night of November's full moon. During the evening, thousands of people go down to the nearest river to float their *kratongs*, small rafts made from a banana palm and decorated with flowers, a candle and incense, in the belief that this will bring them good luck throughout the year.

Opposite: The Vegetarian Festival is a colourful but noisy event with ear-splitting fire crackers constantly being let off.

Above: Placing a donation into the mouth of a Chinese dragon during Vegetarian Festival.

Right: A guitarist performing at the popular Phuket Blues Festival.

King's Cup Regatta

The Phuket King's Cup Regatta is one of Thailand's biggest and most prestigious sporting events. The sailing competition was inaugurated in 1987 to mark the 60th birthday of King Bhumibol, who was once a keen sailor. It has grown from strength to strength so that today, it is Asia's biggest and most successful regatta, attracting top sportsmen and women from around the world. More than 100 yachts, catamarans, dinghies and windsurfers take part in the annual event, held during the first week of December.

Below: Visitors to Phuket can witness world-class sporting action just off Kata Beach.

Right: The one-week sailing event sees hard-fought racing during the day and lively beach parties at night.

Activities

Phuket, Samui and Krabi are renowned for sun, sand and sea. They offer a variety of exciting, water-based activities, such as sailing, fishing and scuba diving, as well as more leisurely pursuits, like golf and yoga.

Sailing

Phuket is an attractive destination for the boating fraternity, as it has excellent mooring facilities at three marinas located on the island's sheltered east coast. Samui now also gets in on the act, with a popular week-long regatta in late May every year. But you don't have to be a yacht owner to enjoy sailing in Thailand. Visitors can take sailing lessons, charter a boat or enjoy a dinner cruise on board a Chinese-style junk.

Big-Game Fishing

The Andaman Sea is renowned as a haven for big-game fishing. Several companies offer chartered day trips visiting Koh Racha Yai and Koh Racha Noi, just two hours sailing from Chalong, but some companies also offer live-on-board excursions lasting from two to seven days to the Similan Islands in search of prized game fish. Depending on the season, sports fishermen can expect to haul in blue marlin, tuna, shark and barracuda. The more ethical companies support a catch-and-release policy.

Diving and snorkelling

Southern Thailand's underwater world attracts scuba divers and snorkellers from around the globe. There are many centres offering dives in the waters around Phuket, Koh Phi Phi, Krabi, the Similan Islands and Koh Tao near Samui.

The Similans are ranked as one of the top ten dive sites in the world. Novice divers can receive excellent tuition at PADI-accredited dive schools while seasoned divers can embark on adventurous live-aboard excursions to spectacular sites. Speciality courses, such as night diving, deep water diving, wreck diving, fish identification and underwater photography, are also available. Diving off the Andaman coast is affected by the weather, and, during the tourist high season from November to April, by the sheer number of divers keen to get in the water. However, it is during this period that the visibility underwater is at its best whereas from April to October, the sea can be choppy and visibility poor.

Golf

Phuket has a reputation as a top golfing destination. World-class clubs include the Blue Canyon Country Club, which is open to non-members and has two award-winning 18-hole courses: the Canyon and the Lakes. Facilities here include luxurious resort accommodation and a spa. In the past, the venue has hosted the Johnnie Walker Classic three times and the Honda Invitational. Other options for golf enthusiasts include Mission Hills with its challenging, 18-hole, Jack Nicklaus-designed course. Golfers can play with a scenic backdrop of rolling hills and sea views before them.

Top: A guest enjoying a private yoga session on the beach at the Banyan Tree Samui.

Left: Phuket is home to several top golf courses, such as the Blue Canyon Country Club, which is open to non-members.

Opposite: Kayaking and snorkelling are popular activities that the whole family can enjoy. Several companies offer kayaking tours, the most famous of which is John Gray's Sea Canoe in Phuket.

Chapter 2: Phuket Island

Over the past three decades, the growth of Phuket as a tourist destination has been phenomenal, attracting tourists from around the world. Key to its popularity are the island's beauty, the diversity of its attractions, and, of course, the people.

Phuket Town

Phuket Town provides the perfect respite from the beach, especially for those who enjoy uncovering Asia's fascinating history and culture. The historic town has a charming area with many well preserved examples of Sino-Portuguese shophouses and mansions that have been given a new lease of life as guesthouses, boutiques, coffee shops and restaurants. Dibuk, Thalang, Phang Nga, Yaowarat and Krabi Roads can be easily explored on foot.

This page and opposite below: Phuket Town is charming and should not be overlooked. It is worth exploring for a couple of days. Highlights include beautiful historic buildings, excellent restaurants and bustling markets.

Opposite above: The Heroines Monument is one of Phuket's landmarks and honours sisters Chan and Mook who are said to have led the fight against invading Burmese troops.

Phuket's Beaches

Visitors to Phuket are spoilt for choice when it comes to glorious beaches but each one has a distinctly different character.

Opposite page: Phuket's most famous and most developed strip is Patong Beach. For some, the two-kilometre (1¼-mile) beach is an essential Phuket experience, for others it's a brash tourist trap and best avoided.

Above: Lined with shops, bars and seafood restaurants, the beach is often crowded with sunbathers and the waters busy with jet skis and speedboats towing parasailers. Patong Beach also has a reputation as the centre of Phuket's vibrant nightlife with rowdy pubs, clubs and go-go bars.

Above: Jung Ceylon at Patong Beach is a popular shopping destination for tourists. It features a food hall, cafés and a supermarket. Other popular shopping venues include Central Festival. There's also a bustling weekend night market in Phuket Town.

Above right: Patong Beach is famous for its seafood restaurants. Diners can tuck into freshly caught crab, tiger prawns, squid, oysters and the local speciality, Phuket lobster.

Opposite: Phuket has many fabulous sunset beaches where visitors can take a romantic stroll or enjoy beachfront dining.

Karon, Kata and Surin

Above: Palm-lined Kata Beach is renowned as one of Phuket's most beautiful and is a popular choice with families. The fabulous stretch of sand is washed by clear waters and the diminutive Koh Bu lies just offshore. Nightlife in Kata is also more family focused.

Left: Located below the foothills north of Kamala, Surin Beach is one of the finest. The small, tree-lined, curving bay and the surrounding hills are dotted with luxurious resorts and top restaurants, which give it an air of exclusivity, and it's a world away from in-your-face Patong.

Opposite: Five kilometres (three miles) south of Patong is Karon, Phuket's second longest beach and the location of several large upmarket resorts. However, they are set back from the beach, leaving the seafront less developed than Patong. It's still a lively beach, though, and has more than its fair share of restaurants and bars as well as a night bazaar packed with tourist trinkets.

Overleaf: From Kata Viewpoint, the three beaches of Karon, Kata and Kata Noi present a spectacular scene.

Nai Ham

Below and right: *The increasingly popular Nai Ham Beach lies just shy of Phuket's southern tip, a short distance from the popular sunset viewpoint of Promthep Cape. During the day, visitors can relax on the beautiful beach or go snorkelling off the rocky outcrops. There's also a cluster of welcoming beachfront restaurants that benefit from a cooling sea breeze.*

Nai Thon and Nai Yang

Left: Nai Thon Beach is a broad stretch of sand towards the north of the island. It is one of Phuket's less developed beaches but is steadily attracting more visitors, thanks in part to the opening of the chic Pullman Phuket Arcadia Naithon Beach hotel, which enjoys fabulous views across the bay.

Left and above: *Nai Yang Beach lies in the north of the island and is the ideal choice for a quiet and relaxing getaway. The lovely curving bay has a wide stretch of sand and is trimmed by trees and small beachfront restaurants serving good Thai food. In recent years, its low-key charms have been discovered and several luxurious resorts such as the Phuket Marriott Resort now line the beach road.*

Chalong Bay

Chalong Bay lies on the eastern side of Phuket, an area that lacks any of the glorious beaches that are plentiful on the western shores. Its sheltered location, however, provides safe anchorage for yachts.

These pages: There are two jetties at Chalong Bay (right) from which many charter boats (left) set sail for destinations including Koh Phi Phi and Phang Nga Bay. There are also a few bars and restaurants in the area. For a panoramic view of the bay (above), take a trip up to Big Buddha on the Nakkerd Hills where the vista is truly spectacular.

Nightlife and Amusements

Of the six beach districts that offer evening entertainment, Patong is the liveliest. Bangla Road and Soi Sunset are packed with bars and western-style nightclubs. The Kata and Karon area is a smaller version of Patong while Rawai at the southern tip of the island is lined with dozens of small and medium-sized bars. Phuket nightlife also provides family-oriented activities with bowling alleys, English language cinemas and a shooting range.

Above and left: Located between Patong's Bangla Road and Beach Road, is the notorious Soi Sea Dragon, home to the majority of Phuket's raunchy go-go bars. Entertainment in the lively street's open-fronted bars goes on into the early hours. There are also many restaurants, souvenir shops and guesthouses in the area.

This page: Simon Cabaret is a hugely popular tourist attraction. It features a cast of lady boys, known in Thai as 'katoey', in an exotic transvestite cabaret with stunning sets and choreography. The theatre is located on Sirirach Road in Patong Beach. The shows are so popular that three performances are held every night. After the show, guests can pose for photographs with the glamorous artistes.

Khao Sok National Park

Situated on the mainland, Khao Sok National Park contains one of the oldest rainforests in the world. A trip to the park makes for a wonderful day of adventure and exploration.

Right: The mountainous terrain is divided by the Sok River. Guides paddle visitors down the river in canoes, pointing out the park's wildlife as they go. Common sightings include hornbills, kingfishers and monkeys.

Below: After lunch, feeding and spending time with elephants is on the agenda. Adventure tours are available lasting from one to five days and can include a stay at The Rainforest Camp, luxury, floating, tented accommodation on Cheow Lam Lake in the centre of Khao Sok National Park.

Wildlife

Located near Thalang town, 22 km (14 miles) from Phuket Town, the Khao Phra Thaeo Forest Reserve covers 22 km² (8½ sq miles) of some of the last remaining virgin forest in Phuket. Home to a number of rare plants and animals, the park has an environmental study centre on site. Wildlife includes barking deer, bears, wild boar, monkeys and gibbons.

Below: Phuket is home to the Gibbon Rehabilitation Project, a research division of the Wild Animal Rescue Foundation of Thailand (WAR). Its work can be seen at the Gibbon Rehabilitation Centre in the eastern part of Khao Phra Thaeo Forest Reserve, close to the Bang Pae Waterfall. Staffed almost entirely by volunteers, the centre takes in gibbons that have been kept as pets or abused as part of the tourist industry and begins the lengthy process of trying to reintroduce them to their natural environment. Volunteer programmes for tourists are available.

Above: The Thai Village and Orchid Farm is a large complex with beautiful gardens that are home to thousands of varieties of orchids and tropical plants. The centre also provides a taste of Thai traditions, such as classical music and dance, and there are elephant shows and Thai boxing demonstrations.

Opposite: Khao Phra Thaeo Forest Reserve has several features including Ton Sai Waterfall. The area around the falls is noted for its beauty. It is also the site of the park headquarters and a small restaurant. The Gibbon Rehabilitation Centre is next door.

Chapter 3: Islands

The azure waters of the Andaman Sea are scattered with emerald islands trimmed with white sand beaches. Despite the high numbers of tourists, it is still possible to find secluded islands and deserted beaches; your own tropical paradise.

Phi Phi Islands

The two islands of Koh Phi Phi Don and Phi Phi Leh are undoubtedly among Thailand's most beautiful destinations. Although the islands' ever-increasing popularity with tourists and the inevitable development that has followed now means that Phi Phi has lost most of its former tranquillity, visitors can't fail to be impressed by the area's natural beauty and crystal-clear waters.

Above and right: Thailand's glorious island destinations are increasingly attracting new markets and you are as likely to see restaurant signs in Russian and Chinese as in English. Each day tour boats from Krabi and Phuket drop anchor in the bay at Phi Phi Don and hordes of day-trippers come ashore.

Above: Many of the islands in southern Thailand are uninhabited but tour companies offer day trips to some of the most beautiful for sunbathing and snorkelling.

Left: The larger of the two islands, Phi Phi Don consists of two massive limestone outcrops bridged by a strip of white sand with beaches on both sides. The southern beach of Ao Ton Sai is the most developed and its beautifully calm bay is a popular spot for boats to drop anchor.

Opposite below: The scenery around Phi Phi Don is comprised of dramatic limestone cliffs and caves which are the nesting sites for swiftlets. They are fiercely protected by the owners of concessions who harvest the highly valuable nests for the Asian delicacy, bird's nest soup.

Koh Lanta Islands

The islands of Koh Lanta Yai and Koh Lanta Noi (*yai* meaning large and *noi* small in Thai) are embraced by the warm waters off Krabi province. The two islands, along with 52 others in the area, were given protected status in 1990 and now form part of the Koh Lanta National Marine Park.

These pages: The smaller of the two islands, Koh Lanta Noi, is undeveloped and it is Koh Lanta Yai that attracts the majority of tourists. The island is 32 km (20 miles) long and six kilometres (3 ¾ miles) wide with a diverse cultural mix of Thai-Muslim, Thai-Chinese and sea gypsies. Visitors can explore the Old Town, a sleepy village of homes, shophouses and restaurants built on stilts over the water. Today, Ban Saladan on the northern tip of the island acts as the main business and commercial centre and is the place where most visitors arrive and depart by ferry. Day trips to the nearby islands of Koh Rok Nok and Koh Rok Nai are popular for snorkelling and sunbathing.

Koh Hong

Above: The scenic coastline around Krabi is particularly beautiful at sunset when fishermen head out to sea and cast their nets onto a shimmering gold sea. Several tour companies and resorts in the area offer sunset boat trips around the many islands.

Right: Koh Hong, or Room Island, lies just off the mainland in Krabi. At the back of the island is a secluded beach which can be reached via long-tail boat from Ao Nang. Within the secluded bay, visitors can step onto pristine sand, swim in calm, crystal-clear waters, and dive down to coral. The beach at Koh Hong is also a popular place for couples to enjoy a romantic Champagne lunch.

Koh Samui

The island of Koh Samui, Thailand's third largest after Phuket and Koh Chang (off the south-eastern coast near the Cambodian border), has a style all of its own. Situated some 700 km (435 miles) south of Bangkok in the Gulf of Thailand and at the edge of the Ang Tong National Marine Park, it is surrounded by 80 other islands, only six of which are inhabited.

Above and left: Living the high life; a guest at the luxurious Banyan Tree Samui enjoying a dip in the private infinity pool while a chef prepares a barbecue on the balcony.

Opposite page: Koh Samui may have started as a backpacker haven but in recent years it has become increasingly known for its high-end luxury resorts.

Left: Mae Nam is one of Koh Samui's quietest and most beautiful beaches. It has an idyllic setting with its stretch of fine yellow sand, lapped by an azure sea, and Koh Pha Ngan visible in the distance.

Below: Chaweng Beach is synonymous with Koh Samui. It may be the longest and most impressive strip of sand on the island but Chaweng is so much more than a beach. It is a destination in itself, a shopper's paradise and the centre of Koh Samui's vibrant nightlife.

Above: Wat Plai Laem is a relatively new temple on Koh Samui. Completed in 2004 and located just one kilometre (two-thirds of a mile) from Big Buddha, it features a beautiful Thai-style 'ubosot' or main temple building. The rest of the design, however, draws upon Chinese Buddhist influences. The expansive grounds include a 20-m (65-ft) high statue of Guanyin, the 18-armed Chinese Goddess of Mercy and Compassion, and a statue of the Chinese fat laughing Buddha which signifies wealth and prosperity. There's also a lake where visitors can release fish and turtles as an act of merit-making. Open from dawn until dusk, the temple gets extremely busy during Chinese festivals.

Left: At the northern tip of the island near Bang Rak Beach, is the Big Buddha. The huge 12-m (39-ft) high golden image was erected in 1972 and has become a symbol of the island.

Chapter 4: Southern Thailand

Below left: *Colourful dresses and sarongs for sale in Ao Nang night market.*

Below: *A traditional fishing boat moored in a Krabi estuary. Fishermen also offer tours for birdwatching in the mangrove forest.*

Beyond Samui and Phuket, the south of Thailand offers incredible natural beauty and an abundance of wildlife that is increasingly attracting adventurous travellers. Krabi is a highlight but provincial, less touristy towns, such as Had Yai and Songkhla, should not be overlooked.

Krabi

Krabi is one of Thailand's top destinations. The idyllic islands and beaches, clear waters, picturesque limestone outcrops, tropical rainforest and protected national parks have gained Krabi a well-deserved reputation as one of the world's most beautiful places. Krabi town is located 814 km (506 miles) south of Bangkok and is served by regular flights from the capital.

Above: The pool at Sofitel Krabi Phokeethra Golf &Spa Resort, one of Krabi's finest hotels.

Left: About 70 km (43 miles) from Krabi Town and near the Khao Phra Bang Khram Nature Reserve are the Nam Tok Ron hot springs where visitors can enjoy bathing in water at a pleasant 35-40°C (95-104°F).

Above: *A fierce image at the entrance of Krabi's Wat Tham Suea, the Tiger Cave Temple.*

Right: *Krabi's limestone mountains are riddled with caves. A ten-minute boat ride from Krabi Town is Khao Khanab Nam Mountain. Here a huge cave features impressive clusters of stalagmites and stalactites. Archaeological excavations have revealed human remains, pottery and prehistoric paintings on the walls. The Japanese army also set up camp in the caves during the Second World War and used it as a base for conducting military operations in the area.*

This page: Tiger Cave Temple is about 3 km (2 miles) from Krabi Town. Inside the cave are what appear to be tiger paw prints in the stone and monks live and worship here. The main attraction is the 1,272-step climb up a limestone tower to a footprint of the Buddha. It's an arduous hike in the heat but once at the top, you are rewarded with stunning, 360-degree views of the surrounding countryside and the Andaman Sea.

Krabi Province

Krabi is a nature lover's paradise though its spectacular scenery, magical underwater world and idyllic islands and beaches mean that tourism is growing quickly.

Above: Ao Nang is Krabi's busiest beach and the centre for shopping and nightlife but so far has not suffered from overdevelopment like Phuket and Koh Samui.

Right and opposite: Railay Beach seen from a hilltop viewpoint. The beach is popular with day-trippers who come for swimming and sunbathing. Get there early and the beach is deserted but by 11 a.m. it's packed. The craggy cliff faces at Railay attract rock climbers from all over the world and it is a good place to learn the sport.

Phang Nga Bay National Park

Phang Nga Bay is home to one of the most distinctive landscapes in Southeast Asia. Here the coast is edged with a tangle of mangrove roots and the blue ocean scattered with emerald limestone islands, weathered by time into unusual shapes. Fleets of tourist boats come here from Phuket but the area is more conveniently reached from Krabi. Attractions include Koh Tapu, or Nail Island, which is now more commonly referred to as James Bond Island. The striking formation was used as a backdrop for a scene in the Bond movie, *The Man with the Golden Gun*, in the 1970s. Elsewhere in the bay there is a Muslim fishing village to explore and fine examples of primitive cave art to see.

These pages: Krabi's limestone scenery is impressive. Boat tours take visitors around dozens of islands and to fishing villages whose inhabitants now rely more on selling trinkets to a steady supply of tourists than they do on bringing in the daily catch.

Opposite top: Koh Tapu, or Nail Island, made famous by the James Bond movie, attracts boatloads of day-trippers. Get there early to avoid the crowds.

Above and right: Fish farming at Koh Panyi. Local Muslim fishermen also farm the local delicacy of Phuket lobster in pens around these waters. The catch is sold to restaurants in Phuket and Krabi.

Opposite: A Muslim fishing village is built on stilts around the island of Koh Panyi. A trip here features on almost all tour itineraries from Phuket and Krabi. The village has a mosque, school, restaurants for visitors and a floating football pitch. Around 100 families make their living from fishing and selling souvenirs. Some families also offer overnight homestays.

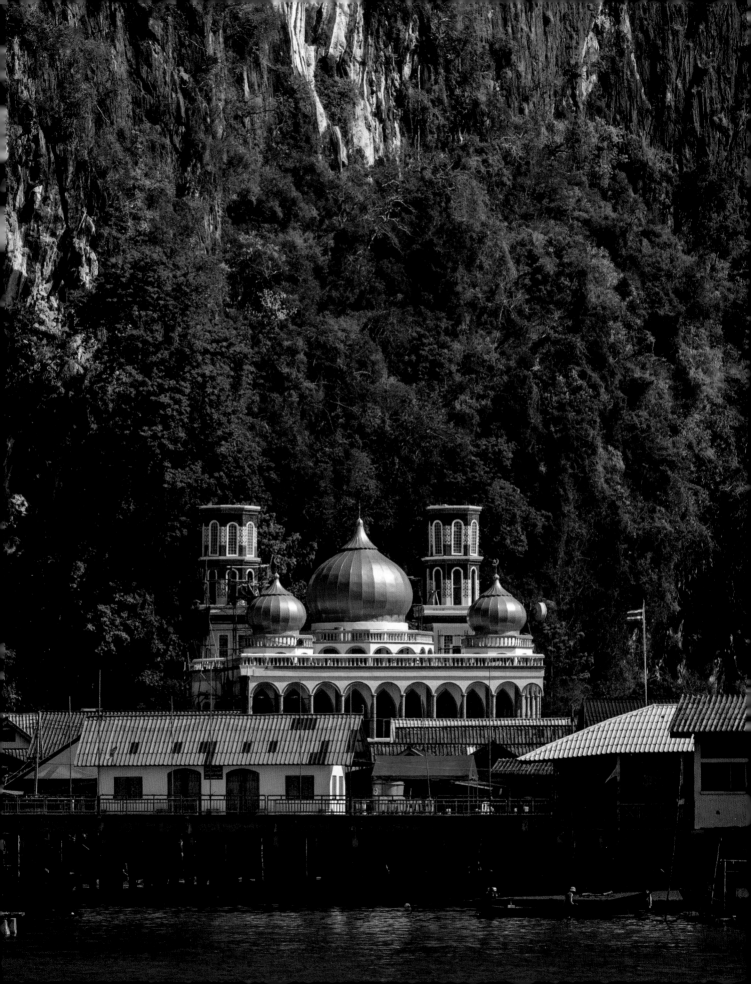

Had Yai

Located in Thailand's far south, Had Yai is the country's fourth largest city and has flourished due to tourism and trade with neighbouring Malaysia. Although the colourful town welcomes few international travellers, it has much to offer, including excellent markets and a huge standing Buddha image perched on a nearby hilltop.

Above: Had Yai can be reached by air or by train from Bangkok. The town is also only a short distance from the border with Malaysia.

Left: Had Yai Municipal Park is an expansive park on a hill overlooking the town. Located 6 km (4 miles) from the town, it is a popular recreational spot for locals and a good place to enjoy sunsets. The main attraction here is the huge standing Buddha image but there is also an image of Guanyin, the Chinese Goddess of Mercy and Compassion, and a short cable-car ride to another hilltop.

Above: Had Yai has several busy fresh markets. Rise early and they are a great way to experience a taste of local life.

Left: From Had Yai, day trips can be made to the port of Songkhla. The small fishing town has some lovely old buildings, great places to eat and a lively market. It also makes a good place for an overnight stay.

Getting About

Phuket, Krabi, Samui and Had Yai airports are all served by daily flights from Bangkok and Chiang Mai, as well as various other domestic and international flights.

Air-conditioned coaches leave for Phuket, Krabi, Samui and Had Yai several times a day from Bangkok's southern bus terminal as well as from other major towns and cities across Thailand.

Online taxi service Grab now serves the main resorts covered in this book, but transportation in Phuket especially can still be problematic. The huge influx in tourists has seen taxi prices shoot up. Held hostage by the outrageous demands, many tourists have no option but to pay the asking price. Always settle the price of your journey before getting into a regular taxi.

As well as taxis, *songtaews*, a type of open-backed truck converted into a small people-carrier, are available in Phuket, Krabi and Samui. A better and cheaper option may be to hire a car or motorcycle for a few days. However, as in most resorts, there is a fair amount of drunkenness and high spirits, and accidents are common.

Above: The islands of southern Thailand can be explored in traditional long-tail fishing boats.

Opposite: For longer journeys between islands larger ferries offer a frequent service. Cancellations are a possibility during rough weather so allow for flexibility in your schedule.

Below: On Phuket and Koh Samui travellers are at the mercy of taxi drivers. Other options include private car or motorcycle hire but driving can be hazardous and accidents are common.

Resources

Contacts

The following websites may include useful information for organizing your trip to southern Thailand.

Tourism Authority of Thailand: www.tourismthailand.org

Richard Barrow, fulltime blogger and Thailand travel expert: www.richardbarrow.com

Bank holidays (Bank of Thailand): www.bot.or.th

Visas and embassies (Thai Ministry of Foreign Affairs): www.mfa.go.th

Airlines

Thai Airways: www.thaiairways.com

Thai Smile: www.thaismileair.com

Nok Air: www.nokair.com

Bangkok Airways: www.bangkokair.com

AirAsia: www.airasia.com

Viet Jet: www.vietjetair.com

Thai Lion Air: www.lionairthai.com

References

A History of Phuket and the Surrounding Region by Colin Robert Mackay, White Lotus 2013

Krabi: Caught in the Spell by Thom Henley, Thai Nature Education 2003

Acknowledgements

Christian Schlegel at Sofitel Krabi Phokeethra Golf and Spa Resort, Remko Kroesen at Banyan Tree Samui, Aticha Pasaprates, Country Head of Indochina at Red Planet Hotels Limited, Richard Mehr of U Sunsuri Phuket, Prompeth Lertratanapreecha, A Waranyoo and all the team at the Tourism Authority of Thailand, and last but not least my thanks to the Princess of Kalasin, Sudarat Ponpangpa, who managed to fall off an elephant but not before I got the shot.

About the Author

Mick Shippen is a freelance writer and award-winning photographer who has been based in Southeast Asia for 15 years. He travels extensively throughout Asia conducting research for articles and taking photographs for local and international newspapers and magazines. He is the author of six other titles in this series: *Enchanting Cambodia, Enchanting Laos, Enchanting Thailand, Enchanting Myanmar, Enchanting Bangkok, Enchanting Chiang Mai and Northern Thailand,* as well as *Presenting Cambodia,* and of *The Traditional Ceramics of South East Asia.*

Mick is also a contributing writer for the books *To Asia with Love, To Myanmar with Love,* and *To Thailand with Love.* He has provided content and images for several leading guidebooks, and his work has also appeared in numerous magazines, the *Bangkok Post,* and the *Australian Sunday Telegraph.* His images are represented by 4CORNERS images and the world's leading food image library, StockFood www.stockfood.co.uk. Images can be viewed at www.mickshippen.com. Twitter @MickShippen.

Index

ASIA BOOKS

Published and Distributed in Thailand by Asia Books Co., Ltd.,
88/9 Soi Samanchan-Barbos, Prakanong, Klongtoey, Bangkok 10110, Thailand
Tel: (66) 2-146-599;; Email: information@asiabooks.com; www.asiabooks.com

This edition published in the United Kingdom in 2024 by John Beaufoy Publishing,
11 Blenheim Court, 316 Woodstock Road, Oxford OX2 7NS, England
www.johnbeaufoy.com

ISBN 978-1-913679-57-6

Designed by Glyn Bridgewater
Cover design by Ginny Zeal
Cartography by William Smuts
Project management by Rosemary Wilkinson

Printed and bound in Malaysia by Times Offset (M) Sdn. Bhd.

Photo credits

Shutterstock.com/saiko3p (p7); Shutterstock.com/sittitap (p8 top); Shutterstock.com/Steven Bostock (p9); Shutterstock.com/slava296 (p35); Shutterstock.com/Adrian Baker (p41); Phuket101.com (p43 top); Shutterstock.com/Browneye (p45 top); Shutterstock.com/thaisign (p45 bottom); Shutterstock.com/Muzhik (p49); Shutterstock.com/Leksele (p51); Shutterstock.com/Hopewell (p60 top); Shutterstock.com/Tuomas Lehtinen (p62 top); Shutterstock.com/Sinn P. Photography (p62 bottom); Shutterstock.com/swissmacky (p63 bottom); Shutterstock.com/skynetphoto (p63 top); Shuttertock.com/Asmida Azman (p74 top right); Shutterstock.com/skyfish (p77 top).

Cover captions and credits

Front cover: 'James Bond Island', Phang Nga Bay © Shutterstock/Preto Perola Back cover, left to right: The huge Buddha at Hat Yai © Mick Shippen, Spectacular sea view from Promthep Cape © Shutterstock.com/Zhukov, Walking on fire at the Vegetarian Festival, Phuket © Mick Shippen, Sino-Portuguese shophouses in Phuket Town © Shutterstock.com/M J Prototype.

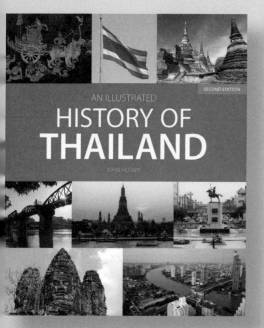

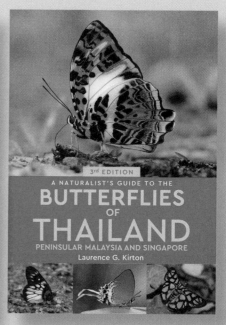
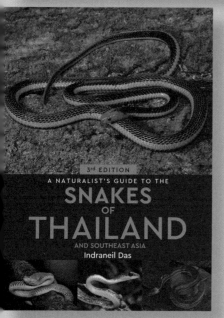

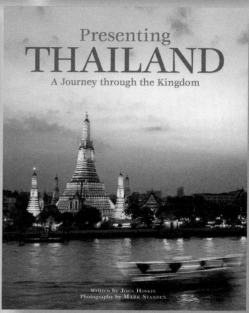